A MONTH OF PRAYER

ST. TERESA
of ÁVILA

A MONTH OF PRAYER

ST. TERESA
_of_ ÁVILA

WYATT NORTH

ISBN 9781647983949

CONTENTS

A Month of Prayer with St. Teresa

INTRODUCTION

Few Christians in history are more revered when it comes to prayer and contemplation than St. Teresa of Ávila. Known for her piety and rapturous mystical experiences, many have sought to pursue her path or a path like it. While some have done this formally in the Carmelite orders she established, countless others have grown in their faith and experiences of intimacy with God through her writings and prayers. This is a humble collection of some of St. Teresa's writings and meditations that form a great foundation for building stronger foundations of prayer with the Holy Spirit's guidance.

DAY 1

In today's meditation, Teresa presents a powerful metaphor for the human soul, particularly with respect to the body and how the whole human being relates to God who seeks to "fill" each person with His presence. As you consider today's meditation, think about how deeply God desires to know you, and what greater intimacy with God might mean for you as you go about your daily life.

Meditations from St. Teresa

I thought of the soul as resembling a castle, formed of a single diamond or a very transparent crystal, and containing many rooms, just as in Heaven there are many mansions.

If we reflect…we shall see that the soul of the just man is but a paradise, in which, God tells us, He takes His delight.

What, do you imagine, must that dwelling be in which a King so mighty, so wise, and so pure, containing in Himself all good, can delight to rest? Nothing can be compared to the great beauty and capabilities of a soul; however keen our intellects may be, they are as unable to comprehend them as to comprehend God, for, as He has told us, He created us in His own image and likeness.

As this is so, we need not tire ourselves by trying to realize all the beauty of this castle, although, being His creature, there is all the difference between the soul and God that there is between the creature and the Creator; the fact that it is made in God's image teaches us how great are its dignity and loveliness. It is no small misfortune and disgrace that, through our own fault, we neither understand our nature nor our origin. Would it not be gross ignorance...if, when a man was questioned about his name, or country, or parents, he could not answer? Stupid as this would be, it is unspeakably more foolish to care to learn nothing of our nature except that we possess bodies, and only to realize vaguely that we have souls, because people say so and it is a doctrine of faith.

Rarely do we reflect upon what gifts our souls may possess, Who dwells within them, or how extremely precious they are. Therefore we do little to preserve their beauty; all our care is concentrated on our bodies, which are but the coarse setting of the diamond, or the outer walls of the castle.

Let us imagine, as I said, that there are many rooms in this castle, of which some are above, some below, others at the side; in the centre, in the very midst of them all, is the principal chamber in which God and the soul hold their most secret intercourse. Think over this comparison very carefully; God grant it may enlighten you about the different kinds of graces He is pleased to bestow upon the soul. No one can know all about them, much less a person so ignorant as I am. The knowledge that such things are possible will console you greatly should our Lord ever grant you.

St. Teresa of Ávila. *The Interior Castle*. First Mansions, Chapter 1.

Additional Biblical Reflections: Psalm 51:10-19, John 14:2, 1 Corinthians 6:19-20.

Prayer

Lord, your majesty is greater than we can possibly comprehend. An entire life of devotion is not enough to know you fully. Grant us, Lord, your Holy Spirit that we might be drawn to you more intimately, that our lives might reflect your glory, and that we would receive your mercy and blessings. Amen.

DAY 2

Nothing can be so perilous in our quest for greater intimacy with God than the tendency we all have to compare our progress to that of others. Truth be told, God does not bestow the same gifts on all of us in the same way. When we allow such comparisons between ourselves and others to creep in, however, we become quickly distracted, consumed with envy, and lose sight of our own spiritual journey. Here, Teresa bids we give thanks to God when He shows special graces to our fellow believers. Rather than being jealous of them, we should take encouragement from the fact that God does, indeed, glorify Himself in His creatures!

Meditations from St. Teresa

I feel sure that vexation at thinking that during our life on Earth God can bestow these graces on the souls of others shows a want of humility and charity for one's neighbour, for why should we not feel glad at a brother's receiving divine favours which do not deprive us of our own share? Should we not rather rejoice at His Majesty's thus manifesting His greatness wherever He chooses? Sometimes our Lord acts thus solely for the sake of showing His power, as He declared when the Apostles questioned whether the blind man whom He cured had been suffering for his own or his parents' sins. God does not bestow these favours on certain souls because they are more holy than others who do not receive them, but to manifest

His greatness, as in the case of St. Paul and St. Mary Magdalen, and that we may glorify Him in His creatures.

St. Teresa of Ávila. *The Interior Castle.* First Mansions, Chapter 1.

Additional Biblical Reflections: Job 5:2, Proverbs 23:17-18, James 3:14-16.

Prayer

Dearest Lord, you are the gracious giver of every good gift. You bestow blessings on your humble creatures according to your infinite well. Grant me a spirit of gratitude for the blessings you show others and spare me from the temptation to grow jealous of how you have chosen to show yourself to others. For you, Lord, are a gracious God who gives to each of us according to your infinite knowledge precisely what is required that we might grow closer to you. Amen.

DAY 3

Today, Teresa warns us against the perils of complacency. Often, when pursuing God, we are tempted to think we have arrived. We have fleeting moments of intimacy and believe the journey is complete. When that happens, Teresa warns, several temptations arise that can destroy our spiritual progress. While we should be content in the graces God has given us, we should never remain complacent or stagnant in our quest toward greater intimacy with the Lord.

Meditations from St. Teresa

This is the deception by which the Devil wins his prey. When a soul finds itself very near to God and sees what a difference there is between the good things of Heaven and those of Earth, and what love the Lord is showing it, there is born of this love a confidence and security that there will be no falling away from what it is now enjoying. It seems to have a clear vision of the reward and believes that it cannot now possibly leave something which even in this life is so sweet and delectable for anything as base and soiled as earthly pleasure. Because it has this confidence, the Devil is able to deprive it of the misgivings which it ought to have about itself; and, as I say, it runs into many dangers, and in its zeal begins to give away its fruit without stint, thinking that it has now nothing to fear. This condition is not a concomitant of pride, for the soul clearly understands that of itself it can do nothing; it is the result of its extreme confidence in God, which knows no discretion. The soul does not realize that it is like a bird still unfledged. It is able to come out of the nest, and God is taking it out, but it is not yet ready to fly, for its virtues are not yet strong and it has no experience which will warn it of dangers, nor is it aware of the harm done by self-confidence.

St. Teresa of Ávila. *A Life.* Chapter 19.

Additional Biblical Reflections: Amos 6:1, Hebrews 6:11-12, Revelation 3:15-17.

Prayer

Lord, you are the great giver of life. As such, you are the giver of growth. Lead us Lord to always seek you more fervently, to desire you more deeply, and to know you more fully. Let us never fall complacent, but make us always content with your blessings and gifts that in all we say and do, we might glorify you through our lives and not be led astray by temptation. In Jesus's name, Amen.

DAY 4

In today's meditation, Teresa bids we consider the mental connection we have to prayer. It is not enough, she says, to simply repeat prayers by rote memory—while our lips move, our minds wander elsewhere. Nor should one speak to the Lord in prayer without forethought, casually as one would to others. The mind should be united to our prayers, whether we vocalize them or not, lest our prayers become exercises in vain repetition rather than conversations with our Divine bridegroom.

Meditations from St. Teresa

As far as I can understand, the gate by which to enter this castle is prayer and meditation. I do not allude more to mental than to vocal prayer, for if it is prayer at all, the mind must take part in it. If a person neither considers to Whom he is addressing himself, what he asks, nor what he is who ventures to speak to God, although his lips may utter many words, I do not call it prayer. Sometimes, indeed, one may pray devoutly without making all these considerations through having practised them at other times. The custom of speaking to God Almighty as freely as with a slave--caring nothing whether the words are suitable or not, but simply saying the first thing that comes to mind from being learnt by rote by frequent repetition – cannot be called prayer: God grant that no Christian may address Him in this manner. I trust His Majesty will prevent any of you, sisters, from doing so. Our habit in this Order of conversing about spiritual matters is a good preservative against such evil ways.

St. Teresa of Ávila. *The Interior Castle.* First Mansions, Chapter 1.

Additional Biblical Reflections: Matthew 6:6-7, Luke 11:1ff, Philippians 4:6

Prayer

Dear Lord, you know the words we would pray even before we speak because you know the groanings of our hearts. Grant that we are given not just the lips but the minds to pray. Guard us against the temptation to turn our prayers into rote repetitions where our voices speak without the concurrence of our hearts so that our prayers might be genuine, fruitful, and pleasing to you. In Jesus's name, Amen.

DAY 5

Teresa often spoke in her autobiography about her own sins. Much like St. Paul, who openly admitted his gravest sins in the first chapters he wrote to the Galatians, Teresa knew that God is glorified not when we hide our shortcomings but when we allow His glory and wisdom to shine through despite our foolishness. False displays of piety merit nothing before God. True confession, an honest assessment of one's sins, and a willingness to accept God's graces in spite of ourselves are what allows us to make spiritual progress. The Lord does not choose to bestow blessings on people solely on account of their merits. He also chooses to bless those of us with certain graces because, in his wisdom, He knows which of us need them the most.

Meditations from St. Teresa

With these few tears that I am here shedding, which are Thy gift (water, in so far as it comes from me, drawn from a well so impure), I seem to be making Thee payment for all my acts of treachery – for the evil that I have so continually wrought and for the attempts that I have made to blot out the favours Thou hast granted me. Do Thou, my Lord, make my tears of some efficacy. Purify this turbid stream, if only that I may not lead others to be tempted to judge me, as I have been tempted to judge others myself. For I used to wonder, Lord, why Thou didst pass by persons who were most holy, who had been piously brought up, who had always served Thee and laboured for Thee and who were truly religious and not, like myself, religious only in name: I could not see why Thou didst not show them the same favours as Thou showedst to me. And then, O my Good, it became clear to me that Thou art keeping their reward to give them all at once – that my weakness needs the help Thou bestowest on me, whereas they, being strong, can serve Thee without it, and that therefore Thou dost treat them as brave souls and as souls devoid of self-seeking.

But nevertheless Thou knowest, my Lord, that I would often cry out unto Thee, and make excuses for those who spoke ill of me, for I thought they had ample reason for doing so. This, Lord, was after Thou of Thy goodness hadst kept me from so greatly offending Thee and when I was turning aside from everything which I thought could cause Thee displeasure; and as I did this, Lord, Thou didst begin to open Thy treasures for Thy servant. It seemed that Thou wert waiting for nothing else than that I should be willing and ready to receive them, and so, after a short time, Thou didst begin, not only to give them, but to be pleased that others should know Thou wert giving them, to me.

St. Teresa of Ávila. *A Life*. Chapter 19.

Additional Biblical Reflections: Luke 5:31, Galatians 1:11-24, Timothy 1:15

Prayer

Lord, you are a God of mercy and grace. In your son, we have been granted the right to approach your throne with confidence. Let us not shy away from confessing our sins, hiding our errors from neither you nor men. That it might be you and your grace rather than our false piety that we uphold before men. In Jesus's name. Amen.

DAY 6

One of the reasons many of us struggle to make any spiritual progress is that we are so *busy*. It is not that we lack the desire to grow in our relationship with the Divine; we simply don't have the time. However, everyone has twenty-four hours in their day. Is it a matter of not having the time? Or fearing that if we give up the time we have devoted to other tasks—especially work—we'll pay financial consequences, perhaps even lose our homes or go hungry? The fear of financial insecurity has bred many in our world who are addicted to work and, in turn, make little time for spiritual reflection. In today's meditation, Teresa speaks to some of her fellow nuns about this very issue.

Meditations from St. Teresa

Do not think, my sisters, that because you do not go about trying to please people in the world you will lack food. You will not, I assure you: never try to sustain yourselves by human artifices, or you will die of hunger, and rightly so. Keep your eyes fixed upon your Spouse: it is for Him to sustain you; and, if He is pleased with you, even those who like you least will give you food, if unwillingly, as you have found by experience. If you should do as I say and yet die of hunger, then happy are the nuns of Saint Joseph's! For the love of the Lord, let us not forget this: you have forgone a regular income; forgo worry about food as well, or thou will lose everything. Let those whom the Lord wishes to live on an income do so: if that is their vocation, they are perfectly justified; but for us to do so, sisters, would be inconsistent.

Worrying about getting money from other people seems to me like thinking about what other people enjoy. However much you worry, you will not make them change their minds nor will they become desirous of giving you alms. Leave these anxieties to Him Who can move everyone, Who is the Lord of all money and of all who possess money. It is by His command that we have come here and His words are true – they cannot fail: Heaven and Earth will fail first. Let us not fail Him, and let us have no fear that He will fail us; if He should ever do so it will be for our greater good, just as the saints failed to keep their lives when they were slain for the Lord's sake, and their bliss was increased through their martyrdom. We should be making a good exchange if we could have done with this life quickly and enjoy everlasting satiety.

St. Teresa of Ávila, *The Way of Perfection*, Chapter 2.

Additional Biblical Reflections: Matthew 6:25-34; Philippians 4:19; 1 Timothy 6:10

Prayer

Dearest Lord, you are the creator of the world and every good thing that we need to sustain us in this body and life. Grant us confidence in your provision, Lord, that we might know that we will never lack any good thing. For as you remind us, man cannot live on bread alone but requires the daily sustenance of your word. Help us in our unbelief that we might devote ourselves more fully to you. Amen.

DAY 7

It is notable that Teresa, when outlining what she believes are the most necessary habits to develop when engaging a contemplative life, focuses first on the love of one another. In today's meditation, she addresses— particularly for nuns in her convent—the tendency for human beings to find each other annoying. Annoyance with our fellow believers can be an insidious thing. We ignore it because we think a mere annoyance is no small thing. However, over time, these nuisances pile up, and we begin to form deep-seated resentments against one another that can be incredibly destructive not only to our own spiritual progress but also to the Church as a whole.

Meditations from St. Teresa

It is about prayer that you have asked me to say something to you. As an acknowledgment of what I shall say, I beg you to read frequently and with a good will what I have said about it thus far, and to put this into practice. Before speaking of the interior life – that is, of prayer – I shall speak of certain things which those who attempt to walk along the way of prayer must of necessity practise. So necessary are these that, even though not greatly given to contemplation, people who have them can advance a long way in the Lord's service, while, unless they have them, they cannot possibly be great contemplatives, and, if they think they are, they are much mistaken. May the Lord help me in this task and teach me what I must say, so that it may be to His glory. Amen.

With regard to the first – namely, love for each other – this is of very great importance; for there is nothing, however annoying, that cannot easily be borne by those who love each other, and anything which causes annoyance must be quite exceptional. If this commandment were kept in the world, as it should be, I believe it would take us a long way towards the keeping of the rest; but, what with having too much love for each other or too little, we never manage to keep it perfectly.

St. Teresa of Ávila, *The Way of Perfection,* Chapter 4.

Additional Biblical Reflections: John 13:34-35, 1 Corinthians 13:1-11, 1 Peter 4:8

Prayer

Lord, in your infinite patience, you bear with us and love us often despite ourselves. Help us, Lord, to have this same disposition toward our fellows and that we not allow minor differences or annoyances to tempt us to sin against each other and, therefore, against you. Teach us to bear one another patiently, in love, and that in our relationships with our fellow believers, we might also come to know you more intimately. Amen.

DAY 8

We should be cautious about wrapping our faith up too tightly with the example of our mentors. Writing to the nuns of her order, Teresa strongly urged them to imitate the Virgin Mother—not her. She is a sinner—too great a one, she says, to be worthy of imitation. This might strike us as odd—particularly when Teresa's piety is so renowned. But her piety came with recognition and acknowledgment of her own sin. We all have mentors in the faith—people whose example we would like to emulate. However, how do we respond when such people let us down, find themselves caught in sin, and fail to be worthy of imitation? Such things should never surprise us. We are all sinners. Perfection eludes even the most pious of the saints! Instead, let us fix our eyes on the Lord.

Meditations from St. Teresa

His Majesty knows that I have nothing to rely upon but His mercy; as I cannot cancel the past, I have no other remedy but to flee to Him, and to confide in the merits of His Son and of His Virgin Mother, whose habit, unworthy as I am, I wear as you do also. Praise Him, then, my daughters, for making you truly daughters of our Lady, so that you need not blush for my wickedness as you have such a good Mother. Imitate her; think how great she must be and what a blessing it is for you to have her for a patroness, since my sins and evil character have brought no tarnish on the lustre of our holy Order.

Still I must give you one warning: be not too confident because you are nuns and the daughters of such a Mother. David was very holy, yet you know what Solomon became. Therefore do not rely on your enclosure, on your penitential life, nor on your continual exercise of prayer and constant communion with God, nor trust in having left the world or in the idea that you hold its ways in horror. All this is good, but is not enough, as I have already said, to remove all fear; therefore meditate on this text and often recall it: 'Blessed is the man that feareth the Lord.'

St. Teresa of Ávila. *The Interior Castle.* Third Mansions, Chapter 1.

Additional Biblical Reflections: 2 Samuel 12, Psalm 51:10-19, Matthew 26:75

Prayer

Lord, we thank you for the great men and women of faith whom you have given us to guide you into the truth. However, let us not turn our mentors into idols. Help us to see them through your eyes even as you look at us in mercy. Let us become imitators of Christ, rather than mimickers of men, that we might ever reflect your holiness more perfectly in our lives. Amen.

DAY 9

In today's world, we often find ourselves chasing a "spiritual high," a fleeting emotion that gives us a sense of God's presence. Teresa does not decry these feelings, but she insists that we should not make too much of them. This "sweetness," as she calls it, comes from us. However, there is a deeper sense, a "spiritual consolation," which may or may not feel sweet but nevertheless comes to us from God and persists even when the luster of the moment fades.

Meditations from St. Teresa

I will now describe, as I promised, the difference between sweetness in prayer and spiritual consolations. It appears to me that what we acquire for ourselves in meditation and petitions to our Lord may be termed 'sweetness in devotion.' It is natural, although ultimately aided by the grace of God. I must be understood to imply this in all I say, for we can do nothing without Him. This sweetness arises principally from the good work we perform, and appears to result from our *labours: well may we feel happy at having thus spent our time. We shall find, on consideration, that many temporal matters give us the same pleasure – such as unexpectedly coming into a large fortune, suddenly meeting with a dearly-loved friend, or succeeding in any important or influential affair which makes a sensation in the world. Again, it would be felt by one who had been told her husband, brother, or son was dead, and who saw him return to her alive. I have seen people weep from such happiness, as I have done myself. I consider both these joys and those we feel in religious matters to be natural ones. Although there is nothing wrong about the former, yet those produced by devotion spring from a more noble source – in short, they begin in ourselves and end in God. Spiritual consolations, on the contrary, arise from God, and our nature feels them and rejoices as keenly in them, and indeed far more keenly, than in the others I described.*

O Jesus! how I wish I could elucidate this point! It seems to me that I can perfectly distinguish the difference between the two joys, yet I have not the skill to make myself understood; may God give it me!

St. Teresa of Ávila. *The Interior Castle.* Fourth Mansions, Chapter 1.

Additional Biblical Reflections: 2 Corinthians 10:5, Philippians 4:5-7, Galatians 5:22-23

Prayer

Dearest Lord, we pray that you grant us genuine spiritual consolations. You made us, Lord, as creatures full of emotions. These emotions are good, and we thank you for them. However, in sin, our emotions often lead us astray. Console us through the Spirit, the great Comforter, that we might find solace in you and not in the pursuit of vain and temporary feelings. Amen.

DAY 10

In today's meditation, Teresa considers how to manage our human tendency to quarrel with one another. First, she emphasizes the importance of refraining from quarrels and taking such matters to prayer. Second, she speaks quite harshly about how quarrelsome individuals must be dealt with. While she is speaking in the context of convents, in truth, the severity of her remedies should give us some pause about how long we are willing to tolerate unnecessary quarrels. Such divisions should be resolved as soon as possible, lest the divide drives a wedge between the members of the body of Christ and deprive all of His presence. Many people are seemingly addicted to conflict. While we should bear with our brothers and sisters who are tempted to quarrel, this tendency must also be addressed.

Meditations from St. Teresa

If one of you should be cross with another because of some hasty word, the matter must at once be put right and you must betake yourselves to earnest prayer. The same applies to the harbouring of any grudge, or to party strife, or to the desire to be greatest, or to any nice point concerning your honour. (My blood seems to run cold, as I write this, at the very idea that this can ever happen, but I know it is the chief trouble in convents.) If it should happen to you, consider yourselves lost. Just reflect and realize that you have driven your Spouse from His home: He will have to go and seek another abode, since you are driving Him from His own house. Cry aloud to His Majesty and try to put things right; and if frequent confessions and communions do not mend them, you may well fear that there is some Judas among you.

For the love of God, let the prioress be most careful not to allow this to occur. She must put a stop to it from the very outset, and, if love will not suffice, she must use heavy punishments, for here we have the whole of the mischief and the remedy. If you gather that any of the nuns is making trouble, see that she is sent to some other convent and God will provide them with a dowry for her. Drive away this plague; cut off the branches as well as you can; and, if that is not sufficient, pull up the roots. If you cannot do this, shut up anyone who is guilty of such things and forbid her to leave her cell; far better this than that all the nuns should catch so incurable a plague. Oh, what a great evil is this! God deliver us from a convent into which it enters: I would rather our convent caught fire and we were all burned alive. As this is so important I think I shall say a little more about it elsewhere, so I will not write at greater length here, except to say that, provided they treat each other equally, I would rather that the nuns showed a tender and affectionate love and regard for each other, even though there is less perfection in this than in the love I have described, than that there were a single note of discord to be heard among them. May the Lord forbid this, for His own sake. Amen.

St. Teresa of Ávila, *The Way of Perfection*, Chapter 7.

Additional Biblical Reflections: Proverbs 15:18, 26:21-28, Mathew 5:22, 2 Timothy 2:23-24

Prayer

Lord, you are a lover of peace and concord. There should never be unsavory divisions in your body. Grant us your Spirit of peace and understanding that we would always be led to view one another with charity, and our Church would be built up through profitable dispute rather than damaged through unnecessary division. Amen.

DAY 11

The pursuit of worldly things can be all-consuming. If this was true in Teresa's day, it is likely an even greater problem now. Some of us pursue material wealth, the latest gadgets and devices, with an unhealthy obsession. Others pursue reputations before men, which leads us to compromise and engender a sense that our "worth" hinges on men's opinions. Still others pursue "success" at all costs and imagine that if we finally achieve a promotion or status, we will find happiness. In today's meditation, Teresa challenges us to reconsider our priorities.

Meditations from St. Teresa

What is there that can be bought with this money which people desire? Is there anything valuable? Is there anything lasting? If not, why do we desire it? It is but a miserable ease with which it provides us and one that costs us very dear. Very often it provides hell for us; it buys us eternal fire and endless affliction. Oh, if all would agree to consider it as useless dross, how well the world would get on, and how little trafficking there would be! How friendly we should all be with one another if nobody were interested in money and honour! I really believe this would be a remedy for everything. The soul sees what blindness there is in the world where pleasures are concerned and how even in this life they purchase only trials and unrest. What disquiet! What discontent! What useless labour! Not only does the soul perceive the cobwebs which disfigure it and its own great faults, but so bright is the sunlight that it sees every little speck of dust, however small; and so, however hard a soul may have laboured to perfect itself, once this Sun really strikes it, it sees that it is wholly unclean. Just so the water in a vessel seems quite clear when the sun is not shining upon it; but the sun shows it to be full of specks. This comparison is literally exact. Before the soul had experienced that state of ecstasy, it thought it was being careful not to offend God and doing all that it could so far as its strength permitted. But once it reaches this stage, the Sun of Justice strikes it and forces it to open its eyes, whereupon it sees so many of these specks that it would fain close them again. For it is not yet so completely the child of that mighty eagle that it can look this Sun full in the face; nevertheless, during the short time that it can keep them open, it sees that it is wholly unclean. It remembers the verse which says: Who shall be just in Thy presence?

St. Teresa of Ávila, *A Life*, Chapter 20.

Additional Biblical Reflections: John 12:42-43, Galatians 1:10, 1 Timothy 6:10

Prayer

Lord, all good things come from you. Help us to have the eyes to see your greater blessings—the treasures you have stored for us in Heaven—without fixating on the treasures of this life. Grant us priorities that mirror your heart that we might always pursue you above worldly wealth, success, or the praises of men. Amen.

DAY 12

Fear is a powerful emotion. When we read about the Devil in the Scriptures, we might be struck with fear. But fear like this proceeds from unbelief. After all, if God is for us, not even the Devil can stand against us. Nevertheless, many are consumed with this kind of fear. The fear of the Devil, or the fear of men, has led many away from God. Teresa here encourages us to take courage in our spiritual battle against the Devil because we have a Champion—our Lord—who fights on our behalf.

Meditations from St. Teresa

This courage which the Lord gave me for my fight with the devils I look upon as one of the great favours He has bestowed upon me; for it is most unseemly that a soul should act like a coward, or be afraid of anything, save of offending God, since we have a King Who is all-powerful and a Lord so great that He can do everything and makes everyone subject to Him. There is no need for us to fear if, as I have said, we walk truthfully in His Majesty's presence with a pure conscience. For this reason, as I have said, I should desire always to be fearful so that I may not for a moment offend Him Who in that very moment may destroy us. If His Majesty is pleased with us, there is none of our adversaries who will not wring his hands in despair. This, it may be said, is quite true, but what soul is upright enough to please Him altogether? It is for this reason, it will be said, that we are afraid. Certainly there is nothing upright about my own soul: it is most wretched, useless and full of a thousand miseries. But the ways of God are not like the ways of men. He understands our weaknesses and by means of strong inward instincts the soul is made aware if it truly loves Him; for the love of those who reach this state is no longer hidden, as it was when they were beginners, but is accompanied by the most vehement impulses and the desire to see God, which I shall describe later and have described already. Everything wearies such a soul; everything fatigues it; everything torments it. There is no rest, save that which is in God, or comes through God, which does not weary it, for it feels its true rest to be far away, and so its love is a thing most evident, which, as I say, cannot be hidden.

St. Teresa of Ávila, *A Life*, Chapter 26.

Additional Biblical Reflections: Isaiah 51:12, Matthew 10:26-28, Hebrews 13:6

Prayer

Dear Lord, you have defeated every enemy—sin, death, and the Devil. Give us not a spirit of fear but a spirit of courage knowing that you have already achieved for us a victory over all forces of evil. Give us the confidence to trek forward in our pursuits of you, despite any threat that might come, and that we might not be dissuaded on our journey toward greater intimacy with you. In Jesus's name. Amen.

DAY 13

Today, there is much discussion about human rights. We see the rights of many violated or feel our own rights have been infringed upon, and rightly sense that an injustice has occurred. However, Teresa bids we reconsider how we approach the question of "rights." In this world, we should expect injustices. This is a broken world. Despite this, though, we have a great example. Our Lord set aside every right that was his by virtue of His Divinity and even had his human rights violated when he was arrested, tortured, and crucified. From Him, we can take comfort in a world where justice is often fleeting.

Meditations from St. Teresa

I often tell you, sisters, and now I want it to be set down in writing, not to forget that we in this house, and for that matter anyone who would be perfect, must flee a thousand leagues from such phrases as: "I had right on my side"; "They had no right to do this to me"; "The person who treated me like this was not right". God deliver us from such a false idea of right as that! Do you think that it was right for our good Jesus to have to suffer so many insults, and that those who heaped them on Him[1] were right, and that they had any right to do Him those wrongs? I do not know why anyone is in a convent who is willing to bear only the crosses that she has a perfect right to expect: such a person should return to the world, though even there such rights will not be safeguarded. Do you think you can ever possibly have to

---

[1] Lit.: "did them to Him."

bear so much that you ought not to have to bear any more? How does right enter into the matter at all? I really do not know.

St. Teresa of Ávila, *The Way of Perfection*, Chapter 13.

Additional Biblical Reflections: Jeremiah 22:3-5, Ecclesiastes 5:8, Romans 12:1-7

Prayer

Dear Lord, you grant us many gifts that the world does not. Send your spirit on all who are oppressed that they might endure in the faith. Give us a heart of gratitude for your gifts rather than a spirit of entitlement for the rights that, while ours, are often denied us. And give us a spirit of patience and confidence in the full knowledge that you will eventually rule over the Earth in perfect justice. In Jesus's name. Amen.

DAY 14

Upon recognizing that we are saved by grace, we may often be tempted to minimize the severity of sin. However, as Teresa points out, while we might be saved despite our sins, the ongoing pursuit of sin can be devastating in our pursuit of God. One cannot expect the Holy Spirit to dwell within us while in the throes of a mortal sin.

Meditations from St. Teresa

While the soul is in mortal sin nothing can profit it; none of its good works merit an eternal reward, since they do not proceed from God as their first principle, and by Him alone is our virtue real virtue. The soul separated from Him is no longer pleasing in His eyes, because by committing a mortal sin, instead of seeking to please God, it prefers to gratify the Devil, the prince of darkness, and so comes to share his blackness. I knew a person to whom our Lord revealed the result of a mortal sin and who said she thought no one who realized its effects could ever commit it, but would suffer unimaginable torments to avoid it. This vision made her very desirous for all to grasp this truth, therefore I beg you, my daughters, to pray fervently to God for sinners, who live in blindness and do deeds of darkness.

In a state of grace the soul is like a well of limpid water, from which flow only streams of clearest crystal. Its works are pleasing both to God and man, rising from the River of Life, beside which it is rooted like a tree. Otherwise it would produce neither leaves nor fruit, for the waters of grace nourish it, keep it from withering from drought, and cause it to bring forth good fruit. But the soul by sinning withdraws from this stream of life, and growing beside a black and fetid pool, can produce nothing but disgusting and unwholesome fruit.

Notice that it is not the fountain and the brilliant sun which lose their splendour and beauty, for they are placed in the very centre of the soul and cannot be deprived of their lustre. The soul is like a crystal in the sunshine over which a thick black cloth has been thrown, so that however brightly the sun may shine the crystal can never reflect it.

O souls, redeemed by the Blood of Jesus Christ, take these things to heart; have mercy on yourselves! If you realize your pitiable condition, how can you refrain from trying to remove the darkness from the crystal of your souls.

St. Teresa of Ávila. *The Interior Castle*. First Mansions, Chapter 2.

Additional Biblical Reflections: 1 Samuel 16:15, John 16:7, 1 Corinthians 3:16, Ephesians 4:30

Prayer

Your Spirit, Lord, is greater than any possession and more satisfying than any sin. Cleanse our hearts, O Lord, and give us strength in temptation that we would not grieve the Spirit but grow ever more deeply in our relationship with you through Your Spirit's indwelling. Amen.

DAY 15

Christianity often gets a "bad rap" for restricting us in our freedom. However, freedom to sin is not genuine freedom; it is bondage. Teresa encourages us to explore within the confines of the great "interior castle" of our prayer lives. We should not restrict God's willingness to show us new blessings and revelations by imposing strict regulations on our forms and habits of prayer.

Meditations from St. Teresa

A soul which gives itself to prayer, either much or little, should on no account be kept within narrow bounds. Since God has given it such great dignity, permit it to wander at will through the rooms of the castle, from the lowest to the highest. Let it not force itself to remain for very long in the same mansion, even that of self-knowledge. Mark well, however, that self-knowledge is indispensable, even for those whom God takes to dwell in the same mansion with Himself. Nothing else, however elevated, perfects the soul which must never seek to forget its own nothingness. Let humility be always at work, like the bee at the honeycomb, or all will be lost. But, remember, the bee leaves its hive to fly in search of flowers and the soul should sometimes cease thinking of itself to rise in meditation on the grandeur and majesty of its God. It will learn its own baseness better thus than by self-contemplation, and will be freer from the reptiles which enter the first room where self-knowledge is acquired. Although it is a great grace from God to practise self-examination, yet 'too much is as bad as too little,' as they say; believe me, by God's help, we shall advance more by contemplating the divinity than by keeping our eyes fixed on ourselves, poor creatures of Earth that we are.

St. Teresa of Ávila. *The Interior Castle.* First Mansions, Chapter 2.

Additional Biblical Reflections: Psalm 119:45, John 8:36, 2 Corinthians 3:17

Prayer

Lord, you are the true source of genuine freedom. Let us not be enslaved to a habit or pattern that leads us to approach you with trepidation or terror. Instead, grant us the freedom to explore your graces in the great Castle of our faith. Amen.

DAY 16

It can often seem like the world is stacked against us, making greater pursuits of God impossible. However, as Teresa reminds us in today's meditation, God often works through human error and even persecution to show us Himself more clearly. In what ways has God used unfortunate circumstances, sorrow, suffering, or even bad advice to accomplish something great in your life?

Meditations from St. Teresa

Whenever the Lord gave me some command in prayer and the confessor told me to do something different, the Lord Himself would speak to me again and tell me to obey Him; and His Majesty would then change the confessor's mind so that he came back and ordered me to do the same thing. When a great many books written in Spanish were taken from us and we were forbidden to read them, I was very sorry, for the reading of some of them gave me pleasure and I could no longer continue this as I had them only in Latin. Then the Lord said to me: "Be not distressed, for I will give thee a living book." I could not understand why this had been said to me, for I had not then had any visions. But a very few days afterwards, I came to understand it very well, for what I saw before me gave me so much to think about and so much opportunity for recollection, and the Lord showed me so much love and taught me by so many methods, that I have had very little need of books – indeed, hardly any. His Majesty Himself has been to me the Book in which I have seen what is true. Blessed be such a Book, which leaves impressed upon us what we are to read and do, in a way that is unforgettable! Who can see the Lord covered with wounds and afflicted with persecutions without embracing them, loving them and desiring them for himself? Who can see any of the glory which He gives to those who serve Him without recognizing that anything he himself can do and suffer is absolutely nothing compared with the hope of such a reward? Who can behold the torments suffered by the damned without feeling that the torments of Earth are by comparison pure joy and realizing how much we owe to the Lord for having so often delivered us from damnation?

St. Teresa of Ávila, *A Life,* Chapter 26.

Additional Biblical Reflections: Matthew 5:10, Luke 6:22, 2 Corinthians 12:10, 2 Timothy 3:12

Prayer

Dear Lord, you told us that those who follow you would invariably bear their crosses after you. Sustain us, Lord, in confidence and in imitation of your Son that with Him, we might pass through the fiery trials of this life and live with You in His resurrection. Amen.

DAY 17

Perspective is important. When we begin complaining to God about how things might not be as we wish, we could do well to heed Teresa's words. Here, Teresa reminds us how incredible it is that God would look upon us in favor after he, too, has seen the depths of our hearts in sin. What a marvel it is, in fact, that God has shown us grace!

Meditations from St. Teresa

O wondrous loving-kindness of God, Who permittest Thyself to be looked upon by eyes which have looked on things as sinfully as have the eyes of my soul! After this sight, Lord, may they never more accustom themselves to look on base things and may nothing content them but Thee. O ingratitude of mortal men! How far will it go? I know by experience that all I am saying now is true and that what it is possible to say is the smallest part of what Thou doest with a soul that Thou leadest to such heights as this. O souls that have begun to pray and that possess true faith, what blessings can you find in this life to equal the least of these, to say nothing of the blessings you may gain in eternity? Reflect – for this is the truth – that to those who give up everything for Him God gives Himself. He is not a respecter of persons He loves us all: no one, however wicked, can be excluded from His love since He has dealt in such a way with me and brought me to so high a state. Reflect that what I am saying is barely a fraction of what there is to say.

St Teresa of Ávila, *A Life,* Chapter 27.

Additional Biblical Reflections: Psalm 103:10-12, Micah 7:18-19, Luke 7:47-48

Prayer

Dear Lord, you bestow many blessings on us in our lives. However, most of all, the greatest wonder and marvel of our faith is that you accept us through the forgiveness merited by Jesus Christ. Help us always to cherish this reality near to our hearts. In Jesus's name. Amen.

DAY 18

We are fickle creatures. How easily do we get distracted by worldly things? Without even realizing it, we often come to realize that somehow, we put our faith on the backburner. Teresa urges us to maintain focus. At the same time, she bids us not to make too much of our sinfulness. We must be repentant but also approach God with what she calls a "holy boldness" that can approach Him in confidence on account of Jesus.

Meditations from St. Teresa

O Lord! All our trouble comes to us from not having our eyes fixed upon Thee. If we only looked at the way along which we are walking, we should soon arrive; but we stumble and fall a thousand times and stray from the way because, as I say, we do not set our eyes on the true Way. One would think that no one had ever trodden it before, so new is it to us. It is indeed a pity that this should sometimes happen. I mean, it hardly seems that we are Christians at all or that we have ever in our lives read about the Passion. Lord help us – that we should be hurt about some small point of honour! And then, when someone tells us not to worry about it, we think he is no Christian. I used to laugh – or sometimes I used to be distressed – at the things I heard in the world, and sometimes, for my sins, in religious Orders. We refuse to be thwarted over the very smallest matter of precedence: apparently such a thing is quite intolerable. We cry out at once: "Well, I'm no saint"; I used to say that myself.

God deliver us, sisters, from saying "We are not angels", or "We are not saints", whenever we commit some imperfection. We may not be; but what a good thing it is for us to reflect that we can be if we will only try and if God gives us His hand! Do not be afraid that He will fail to do His part if we do not fail to do ours. And since we come here for no other reason, let us put our hands to the plough, as they say. Let there be nothing we know of which it would be a service to the Lord for us to do, and which, with His help, we would not venture to take in hand. I should like that kind of venturesomeness to be found in this house, as it always increases humility. We must have a holy boldness, for God helps the strong, being no respecter of persons; and He will give courage to you and to me.

St. Teresa of Ávila, *The Way of Perfection*, Chapter 16.

Additional Biblical Reflections: Proverbs 4:25, Colossians 3:2, Hebrews 12:2

Prayer

Lord, keep our eyes ever fixed on you. We live in a world full of shiny things that often distract us and send us astray. May your presence always be a reminder of the wonder and luster of your true nature and grace. In Jesus's name. Amen.

DAY 19

It is almost like we look at the world and our lives through distorted lenses. We often amplify the seriousness of earthly matters while minimizing the true impact that God's presence can have on our lives. It is like examining life through the convex side of a spoon, and everything is inverted. Here, Teresa encourages us to recognize that the trivial matters that stress us out in this life mean very little compared to God's glory.

Meditations from St. Teresa

On various occasions it happened that I found myself greatly tried and maligned about a certain matter, to which I shall refer later, by almost everyone in the place where I am living and by my Order. I was greatly distressed by the numerous things which arose to take away my peace of mind. But the Lord said to me: "Why dost thou fear? Knowest thou not that I am all-powerful? I will fulfil what I have promised thee." And shortly afterwards this promise was in fact completely fulfilled. But even at that time I began at once to feel so strong that I believe I could have set out on fresh undertakings, even if serving Him had cost me further trials and I had had to begin to suffer afresh. This has happened so many times that I could not count them. Often He has uttered words of reproof to me in this way, and He does so still when I commit imperfections, which are sufficient to bring about a soul's destruction. And His words always help me to amend my life, for, as I have said, His Majesty supplies both counsel and remedy.

At other times the Lord recalls my past sins to me, especially when He wishes to grant me some outstanding favour, so that my soul feels as if it is really at the Judgment; with such complete knowledge is the truth presented to it that it knows not where to hide. Sometimes these locutions warn me against perils to myself and to others, or tell me of things which are to happen three or four years hence: there have been many of these and they have all come true – it would be possible to detail some of them. There are so many signs, then, which indicate that these locutions come from God that I think the fact cannot be doubted.

St. Teresa of Ávila, *A Life*, Chapter 26.

Additional Biblical Reflections: Isaiah 26:3, John 16:33, 2 Thessalonians 3:16

Prayer

Dearest Lord, you are a God of peace. You desire not only peace in the world but also peace within our hearts. May your presence give us such a sense of peace that we cannot be unsettled by the concerns of this life. In Jesus's name. Amen.

DAY 20

Teresa reminds us, here, that there is no single way to pray that is necessarily guaranteed to produce the same results no matter who prays it. We are all unique, and our relationships with God—while universally defined in terms of Christ—are likewise unique. Accordingly, we should be willing to explore different ways of praying and determine what forms are most beneficial regarding our spiritual growth.

Meditations from St. Teresa

I myself spent over fourteen years without ever being able to meditate except while reading. There must be many people like this, and others who cannot meditate even after reading, but can only recite vocal prayers, in which they chiefly occupy themselves and take a certain pleasure. Some find their thoughts wandering so much that they cannot concentrate upon the same thing, but are always restless, to such an extent that, if they try to fix their thoughts upon God, they are attacked by a thousand foolish ideas and scruples and doubts concerning the Faith. I know a very old woman, leading a most excellent life – I wish mine were like hers – a penitent and a great servant of God, who for many years has been spending hours and hours in vocal prayer, but from mental prayer can get no help at all; the most she can do is to dwell upon each of her vocal prayers as she says them. There are a great many other people just like this; if they are humble, they will not, I think, be any the worse off in the end, but very much in the same state as those who enjoy numerous consolations. In one way they may feel safer, for we cannot tell if consolations come from God or are sent by the Devil. If they are not of God, they are the more dangerous; for the chief object of the Devil's work on Earth is to fill us with pride. If they are of God, there is no reason for fear, for they bring humility with them, as I explained in my other book at great length.

Others walk in humility, and always suspect that if they fail to receive consolations the fault is theirs, and are always most anxious to make progress. They never see a person shedding a tear without thinking themselves very backward in God's service unless they are doing the same, whereas they may perhaps be much more advanced. For tears, though good, are not invariably signs of perfection; there is always greater safety in humility, mortification, detachment and other virtues. There is no reason for fear, and you must not be afraid that you will fail to attain the perfection of the greatest contemplatives.

St. Teresa of Ávila, *The Way of Perfection*, Chapter 17.

Additional Biblical Reflections: Psalm 139:14, Matthew 10:30, Romans 12:1-21

Prayer

Lord, each one of us is the product of your masterful workmanship. Help us to find the ways that befit our constitution and aid us in prayer most effectively. Grant this that we might not fall into vain repetition or meaningless habits, but that our prayer lives will be rich and full as we mature in our faith. Amen.

DAY 21

There is no great sage or saint who provides for us a better model to imitate in the manner of prayer than Jesus. Here, Teresa bids we simply turn to the Gospels and examine how Jesus prayed so that we might learn from His perfect example.

Meditations from St. Teresa

It is always a great thing to base your prayer on prayers which were uttered by the very lips of the Lord. People are quite right to say this, and, were it not for our great weakness and the lukewarmness of our devotion, there would be no need for any other systems of prayer or for any other books at all. I am speaking to souls who are unable to recollect themselves by meditating upon other mysteries, and who think they need special methods of prayer; some people have such ingenious minds that nothing is good enough for them! So I think I will start to lay down some rules for each part of our prayer – beginning, middle and end – although I shall not spend long on the higher stages. They cannot take books from you, and, if you are studious and humble, you need nothing more.

I have always been fond of the words of the Gospels and have found more recollection in them than in the most carefully planned books – especially books of which the authors were not fully approved, and which I never wanted to read. If I keep close to this Master of wisdom, He may perhaps give me some thoughts which will help you. I do not say that I will explain these Divine prayers, for that I should not presume to do, and there are a great many explanations of them already. Even were there none, it would be ridiculous for me to attempt any. But I will write down a few thoughts on the words of the Paternoster; for sometimes, when we are most anxious to nurture our devotion, consulting a great many books will kill it. When a master is himself giving a lesson, he treats his pupil kindly and likes him to enjoy being taught and does his utmost to help him learn. Just so will this heavenly Master do with us.

St. Teresa of Ávila, *The Way of Perfection*, Chapter 21.

Additional Biblical Reflections: Matthew 14:23, Luke 9:28-29, John 11:41-42

Prayer

Lord, how often do we look for wisdom in worldly examples when you have already provided all that we need. Thank you for the example of your Son, Jesus Christ, who not only taught us to pray but also showed us how to pray by his example. Grant that we might follow his lead and more perfectly draw near to you in the same way. Amen.

DAY 22

Are you holding back any sins that you have not yet been willing to confess? In today's meditation, Teresa tells the story of a fellow she counseled who had done exactly that and much to his peril. However, once he confessed his sin, he experienced great freedom and finally experienced greater intimacy with God.

Meditations from St. Teresa

A person came to me who for two and a half years had been living in mortal sin – one of the most abominable sins that I had ever heard of – and during the whole of that time he neither confessed it nor amended his life, and yet went on saying Mass. And, though he confessed his other sins, when it came to that one, he would ask himself how he could possibly confess such a dreadful thing. He had a great desire to give it up but could not bring himself to do so. I was terribly sorry for him and very much distressed to find that God was being offended in such a way. I promised him that I would pray earnestly to God that He would help him and that I would get other people better than myself to do so too, and I wrote to a certain person who, he said, would be able to distribute the letters. And, lo and behold, at the first possible moment, he confessed; for through the many most saintly persons who at my request had prayed to Him on his behalf God was pleased to bestow this mercy upon his soul, and I, miserable though I am, had done what I could and taken the greatest pains about it. He wrote to me and said that he was now so much better that days passed without his falling into this sin, but he was suffering such tortures from temptation that his distress made him feel as if he were already in hell; and he asked me to commend him to God. I spoke about it again to my sisters, through whose prayers the Lord must have granted me this favour, and they took it very much to heart.

St. Teresa of Ávila, *A Life*, Chapter 31.

Additional Biblical Reflections: Proverbs 28:13, 1 John 1:9, James 5:16

Prayer

Lord, there is no such thing as a secret sin in your sight. May we never withhold sins from confession. Instead, lead us to approach you in both humility and repentance but in the confidence of your grace. For you desire not that we would remain burdened by our sins but freed to live lives in greater pursuit of you. Amen.

DAY 23

There are two main thoughts in today's meditation. First, Teresa encourages us to spend time with persons who are more mature in the faith to benefit from their example. Second, she encourages us not to turn our prayer life into a mere "means to an end" of what we have imagined for ourselves. Prayer is not just a "tool" to use to get something better; it is, itself, the great prize.

Meditations from St. Teresa

It is of the utmost importance for the beginner to associate with those who lead a spiritual life, and not only with those in the same mansion as herself, but with others who have travelled farther into the castle, who will aid her greatly and draw her to join them. The soul should firmly resolve never to submit to defeat, for if the devil sees it staunchly determined to lose life and comfort and all that he can offer, rather than return to the first mansion, he will the sooner leave it alone.

Let the Christian be valiant; let him not be like those who lay down to drink from the brook when they went to battle (I do not remember when). Let him resolve to go forth to combat with the host of demons, and be convinced that there is no better weapon than the cross. I have already *said, yet it is of such importance that I repeat it here: let no one think on starting of the reward to be reaped: this would be a very ignoble way of commencing such a large and stately building. If built on sand it would soon fall down.* Souls *who acted thus would continually suffer from discouragement and temptations, for in these mansions no manna rains; farther on, the soul is pleased with all that comes, because it desires nothing but what God wills.*

St. Teresa of Ávila. *The Interior Castle.* Second Mansions.

Additional Biblical Reflections: Proverbs 13:20, Jeremiah 14:7-9, 1 Corinthians 11:1

Prayer

Lord, surround us with giants of faith who might encourage us in our pursuits of you. While we know we should never forget that these men and women are sinners, too, you nonetheless bless our fellow Christians with many gifts from which we might learn and grow. Fill our lives with such people so that we might pray unto you more—not so that we might achieve a particular goal, but because, in prayer, we come to relish in your presence. Amen.

DAY 24

In today's meditation, Teresa encourages proper reverence when we pray. There is a fine balance. We do not want to be so fearful that we worry about the missteps we might make or our choice of words. However, neither do we want to approach God as if he were any man.

Meditations from St. Teresa

When you approach God, then, try to think and realize Whom you are about to address and continue to do so while you are addressing Him. If we had a thousand lives, we should never fully understand how this Lord merits that we behave toward Him, before Whom even the angels tremble. He orders all things and He can do all things: with Him to will is to perform. It will be right, then, daughters, for us to endeavour to rejoice in these wondrous qualities of our Spouse and to know Whom we have wedded and what our lives should be. Why, God save us, when a woman in this world is about to marry, she knows beforehand whom she is to marry, what sort of a person he is and what property he possesses. Shall not we, then, who are already betrothed, think about our Spouse, before we are wedded to Him and He takes us home to be with Him? If these thoughts are not forbidden to those who are betrothed to men on Earth, how can we be forbidden to discover Who this Man is, Who is His Father, what is the country to which He will take me, what are the riches with which He promises to endow me, what is His rank, how I can best make Him happy, what I can do that will give Him pleasure, and how I can bring my rank into line with His.

If a woman is to be happy in her marriage, it is just those things that she is advised to see about, even though her husband be a man of very low station.

St. Teresa of Ávila, *The Way of Perfection,* Chapter 22.

Additional Biblical Reflections: Exodus 3:5, Proverbs 1:7, Hebrews 12:28

Prayer

Lord, we revere your Holy name. For while you desire greater intimacy with us, let us never grow arrogant in our disposition toward you. Grant that we might ever keep your name Holy in all that we say and do. Amen.

DAY 25

When it comes to new Christians or beginners in the habit of prayer, there is a great danger that we might imagine our initial excitement to be regularly expected. In truth, a life in prayer and contemplation—as a way of pursuing Christ—is bound to be accompanied by trials and feelings of "dryness." Teresa encourages us in today's meditation to find Christ precisely in such moments.

Meditations from St. Teresa

What a farce it is! Here are we, with a thousand obstacles, drawbacks, and imperfections within ourselves, our virtues so newly born that they have scarcely the strength to act (and God grant that they exist at all!) yet we are not ashamed to expect sweetness in prayer and to complain of feeling dryness.

Do not act thus, sisters; embrace the cross your Spouse bore on His shoulders; know that your motto should be: 'Most happy she who suffers most if it be for Christ!' All else should be looked upon as secondary: if our Lord give it you, render Him grateful thanks. You may imagine you would be resolute in enduring external trials if God gave you interior consolations: His Majesty knows best what is good for us; it is not for us to advise Him how to treat us, for He has the right to tell us that we know not what we ask. Remember, it is of the greatest importance – *the sole aim of one beginning to practise prayer should be to endure trials, and to resolve and strive to the utmost of her power to conform her own will to the will of God. Be certain that in this consists all the greatest perfection to be attained in the spiritual life, as I will explain later. She who practises this most perfectly will receive from God the highest reward and is the farthest advanced on the right road. Do not imagine that we have need of a cabalistic formula or any other occult or mysterious thing to attain it our whole welfare consists in doing the will of God. If we start with the false principle of wishing God to follow our will and to lead us in the way we think best, upon what firm foundation can this spiritual edifice rest?*

St Teresa of Ávila, *The Interior Castle,* Second Mansions.

Additional Biblical Reflections: John 16:33, Romans 5:3-5, James 1:2-4

Prayer

Lord, you endured suffering and the cross on our behalf. Now, when we engage in trials and suffering of any kind, we can be sure that we will find you in the midst of it. Gather us unto you in your suffering so that we might also be born again with you in your resurrection life. Amen.

DAY 26

Like Jesus, Teresa warns against the spiritual entrapping associated with wealth. She encourages us, who have been blessed, to show charity toward others and give out of our abundance.

Meditations from St. Teresa

A rich man, without son or heir, loses part of his property, but still has more than enough to keep himself and his household. If this misfortune grieves and disquiets him as though he were left to beg his bread, how can our Lord ask him to give up all things for His sake? This man will tell you he regrets losing his money because he wished to bestow it on the poor.

I believe His Majesty would prefer me to conform to His will, and keep peace of soul while attending to my interests, to such charity as this. If this person cannot resign himself because God has not raised him so high in virtue, well and good: let him know that he is wanting in liberty of spirit; let him beg our Lord to grant it him, and be rightly disposed to receive it. Another person has more than sufficient means to live on, when an opportunity occurs for acquiring more property: if it is offered him, by all means let him accept it; but if he must go out of his way to obtain it and then continues working to gain more and more – however good his intention may be (and it must be good, for I am speaking of people who lead prayerful and good lives), he cannot possibly enter the mansions near the King.

St Teresa of **Á**vila, *The Interior Castle,* Third Mansions, Chapter 2.

Wyatt North

Additional Biblical Reflections: Matthew 25:40, Philippians 2:4-8, 1 John 3:17

Prayer

Lord, you bless many of us with material goods and abundance. Protect us from turning these things, which come from you, into false gods. Grant us opportunities to share with others the blessings you have given us. Introduce us to those in need so that we might become your vessel of provision to others you love. In Jesus's name. Amen.

52

DAY 27

How one spends his or her time shows much about where one's heart is. What is "time," though to God, who is eternal? Does God covet our time? Teresa bids we consider the time we offer to God much like a husband might view his ring. While it might be worth relatively little, its worth comes in what it stands for and represents. Our time, likewise, does not add anything to God's character since he lacks nothing. Rather, by giving Him our time in prayer and devotion, we memorialize and live out our relationship with Him.

Meditations from St. Teresa

What wife is there who, after receiving many valuable jewels from her husband, will not give him so much as a ring – which he wants, not because of its value, for all she has is his, but as a sign of love and a token that she will be his until she dies? Does the Lord deserve less than this that we should mock Him by taking away the worthless gift which we have given Him? Since we have resolved to devote to Him this very brief period of time – only a small part of what we spend upon ourselves and upon people who are not particularly grateful to us for it – let us give it Him freely, with our minds unoccupied by other things and entirely resolved never to take it back again, whatever we may suffer through trials, annoyances or aridities. Let me realize that this time is being lent to me and is not my own, and feel that I can rightly be called to account for it if I am not prepared to devote it wholly to God.

St. Teresa of Ávila, *The Way of Perfection,* Chapter 23.

Additional Biblical Reflections: Mark 7:6, Ephesians 1-33, 2 Thessalonians 3:6

Prayer

Dear Lord, you lack nothing, and there is nothing we can add to improve upon your glory. Let us see our gifts and our time, which we offer unto you, not as a gift you require but as a token of our love. Return these offerings, and we bid you with an abundance of your Spirit and presence. Amen.

DAY 28

We are often blind to our faults while we seem to see the faults of others magnified as if through binoculars. Today, Teresa bids we first consider our own faults and sins before we fixate on the flaws and faults of others.

Meditations from St. Teresa

Let us look at our own faults, and not at other persons'. People who are extremely correct themselves are often shocked at everything they see; however, we might often learn a great deal that is essential from the very persons whom we censure. Our exterior comportment and manners may be better--this is well enough, but not of the first importance. We ought not to insist on every one following in our footsteps, nor to take upon ourselves to give instructions in spirituality when, perhaps, we do not even know what it is. Zeal for the good of souls, though given us by God, may often lead us astray, sisters; it is best to keep our rule, which bids us ever to live in silence and in hope. Our Lord will care for the souls belonging to Him; and if we beg His Majesty to do so, by His grace we shall be able to aid them greatly. May He be for ever blessed!

St. Teresa of Ávila, *The Interior Castle,* Third Mansions, Chapter 2.

Additional Biblical Reflections: Isaiah 53:5-6, Matthew 7:1-5, James 4:11-12

Prayer

Lord, we know that all have sinned and fall short of our glory. Grant that we might always have the eyes to see our sins and the confidence to confess them before God and men so that we might be assured of your absolution. Let us not judge others, for it is not our place to judge, but grant us the patience to bear with our fellow brothers and sisters after the pattern of patience you first demonstrated to us. Amen.

DAY 29

In today's meditation, Teresa not only reminds us that persecution and martyrdom are likely in this world, but she also encourages us to pray for others who might be weaker in the faith, so they might stand firm under the pressures of toil and tribulation.

Meditations from St. Teresa

For a soul which God allows to walk in this way in the sight of the whole world may well prepare itself to be martyred by the world, for, if it will not die to the world of its own free will, the world itself will kill it. Really, I can see nothing in the world that seems to me good save its refusal to allow that good people can ever do wrong and the way it perfects them by speaking ill of them. I mean that more courage is necessary for following the way of perfection, if one is not perfect, than for suddenly becoming a martyr; for perfection cannot be acquired quickly, except by one to whom by some particular privilege the Lord is pleased to grant this favour. When the world sees anyone setting out on that road it expects him to be perfect all at once and detects a fault in him from a thousand leagues' distance; yet in that particular person the fault may be a virtue, and his critic, in whom it is a vice, may be judging him by himself. They will not allow him to eat or sleep — they will hardly let him breathe, as we say: the more highly they think of him, the more they seem to forget that he is still in the body. For, however perfect his soul may be, he is still living on Earth, and however resolutely he may trample Earth's miserable limitations beneath his feet, he

57

is still subject to them. And so, as I say, he needs great courage. His poor soul has not yet begun to walk, and men expect it to fly. He has not yet conquered his passions, and men expect him to rise to great occasions and be as brave as they read the saints were after they had been confirmed in grace. What happens here gives us cause for praising the Lord and also for great sorrow of heart, since so many poor souls turn back because they have no idea what to do to help themselves. And I believe my soul would have been like them had not the Lord Himself had such compassion on me and done everything for me. Until He of His goodness had done everything, I myself did nothing, as Your Reverence will know, but fall and rise again.

St. Teresa of Ávila, *A Life*, Chapter 31.

Additional Biblical Reflections: John 15:19, Acts 14:22, Romans 8:35, 1 Peter 3:16

Prayer

Lord, be with all those who are persecuted in both our communities and around the world. Sustain them with the consolations of your Spirit so that their sufferings might also bear witness to you and your glory. In Jesus's name. Amen.

DAY 30

In today's mediation, Teresa offers a prayer unto the Lord, honoring his faithfulness despite our faithlessness. We would do well to imitate Teresa in this way—praising Christ's virtues while recognizing our needs in His presence.

Meditations from St. Teresa

Behold, my Lord, with the love that Thou hast for us and with Thy humility, nothing can be an obstacle to Thee. And then, Lord, Thou hast been upon Earth and by taking our nature upon Thee hast clothed Thyself with humanity: Thou hast therefore some reason to care for our advantage. But behold, Thy Father is in Heaven, as Thou hast told us, and it is right that Thou shouldst consider His honour. Since Thou hast offered Thyself to be dishonoured by us, leave Thy Father free. Oblige Him not to do so much for people as wicked as I, who will make Him such poor acknowledgment.

O good Jesus! How clearly hast Thou shown that Thou art One with Him and that Thy will is His and His is Thine! How open a confession is this, my Lord! What is this love that Thou hast for us? Thou didst deceive the Devil, and conceal from him that Thou art the Son of God, but Thy great desire for our welfare overcomes all obstacles to Thy granting us this greatest of favours. Who but Thou could do this, Lord? I cannot think how the Devil failed to understand from that word of Thine Who Thou wert, beyond any doubt. I, at least, my Jesus, see clearly that Thou didst speak as a dearly beloved son both for Thyself and for us, and Thou hast such power that what Thou sayest in Heaven shall be done on Earth. Blessed be Thou for ever, my Lord, Who lovest so much to give that no obstacle can stay Thee.

St. Teresa of Ávila, *The Way of Perfection*, Chapter 27.

Additional Biblical Reflections: Proverbs 22:4, Matthew 5:2-11, Luke 14:11.

Prayer

Dear Lord, we thank you for the many blessings and graces you have poured upon our lives. Continue to nurture us in your Word that we might come to know you more, pray to you more frequently, and represent your Son more faithfully. In His name. Amen.

www.ingramcontent.com/pod-product-compliance
Lightning Source LLC
Chambersburg PA
CBHW030524100426
42813CB00001B/138